THE
NERVOUS
SYSTEM

Shirley Duke

Rourke
Educational Media

rourkeeducationalmedia.com

Teacher Notes available at
rem4teachers.com

www.rourkeeducationalmedia.com

PHOTO CREDITS: Cover: © michelangelus; Title Page: © Sebastian Kaulitzki; Page 2,3: © ktsimage; Page 4: © ARENA Creative, Sebastian Kaulitzki; Page 5: © Sebastian Kaulitzki, Alila07; Page 6: © Alxhar; Page 7: © Sergey Panteleev; Page 8: © Don Bayley; Page 9: © Legger, Alxhar; Page 10: © Max Delson Martins Santos; Page 11: © Library of Congress, Guido Vrola; Page 12: © Guido Vrola; Page 13: © Medical Art Inc, Cammeraydave; Page 14: © JazzIRT, Mark Bowden, jo unruh; Page 15: © Christopher Futcher; Page 16: © David Marchal; Page 17: © David Marchal, ericsphotography; Page 18: Riccardo Cova; Page 19: © Legger; Page 20: © Sebastian Kaulitzki, Legger; Page 21: © Simon Phipps, Max Delson Martins Santos; Page 22: © Simone Becchetti, Mark Goddard; Page 23: © Andreus; Page 24: © -Oxford-, Matthew Valentine, Sawayasu Tsuji, Stockphoto4u; Page 25: © Andrei Nacu, Medical Art Inc; Page 26: © Chee Ming Wong, KATARZYNA ZWOLSKA; Page 27: © Alila07, Loretta Hostettler; Page 28: © Alberto Pomares, Alegria111; Page 29: © Wikipedia, Patrick J. Lynch, paul kline; Page 30: © JazzIRT; Page 31: © James Boardman, Alila07; Page 32: © Dean Mitchell; Page 33: © RosicaSabotanova, Sura Nualpradid; Page 34: © Henrik Jonsson, Medical Art Inc; Page 35: © Photowitch, Mikhail Kokhanchikov, George Olsson, erwo1; Page 36: © AP IMAGES: DAMIAN DOVARGANES, Parrypix; Page 37: © Konstantin Sutyagin, FotografiaBasica; Page 38: © bojan fatur; Page 39: © AP Images; Page 40: © airportrait; Page 41: © NIMH, kali9; Page 42: © annedde; Page 43: © Semnic, Catherine Yeulet; Page 44: © michelangelus; Page 45: © Daniel Bendjy

Edited by Precious McKenzie

Cover design by Teri Intzegian
Interior layout by Tara Raymo

Library of Congress PCN Data

The Nervous System / Shirley Duke
ISBN 978-1-61810-121-1 (hard cover)
ISBN 978-1-61810-254-6 (soft cover)
Library of Congress Control Number: 2011945265

Rourke Educational Media
Printed in the United States of America,
North Mankato, Minnesota

rourkeeducationalmedia.com

ustomerservice@rourkeeducationalmedia.com • PO Box 643328 Vero Beach, Florida 32964

TABLE OF CONTENTS

Ch 1   Parts of the Nervous System 4

Ch 2   The Brain 8

Ch 3   The Spinal Cord 16

Ch 4   The Senses 22

Ch 5   When Things Go Wrong 30

Ch 6   For the Future 38

Glossary. 46

Index 48

PARTS OF THE NERVOUS SYSTEM

Hop on a skateboard and push off. Eyes, arms, legs, and muscles must coordinate to stay balanced and keep moving. How is this possible? Humans have a complex command center to run the body called the nervous system.

The brain, **spinal cord**, and nerves form the nervous system. This system receives, interprets, and relays information to manage and direct everything happening in the body. Electrical signals called **impulses** carry information. They move from the body to the brain and back again.

Did You Know?

Living organisms develop in an ordered way. The smallest unit of life is a cell. Like cells doing the same job form tissues. Tissues working together make an organ. Organs working together on the same process create a system. All the different systems working together make an organism.

The nervous system is divided into two parts. The brain and spinal cord make up the central nervous system (CNS). The **peripheral nervous system** (PNS) is all the nerves outside the brain and spinal cord. The nerves of the PNS connect the sense organs and other body activities to the CNS.

Messages move through **neurons**, or nerve cells. Bodies hold around 100 billion neurons. Another 100 billion neurons make up the brain. The impulses from these cells move in different directions to carry their messages. Bundles of neurons form nerves.

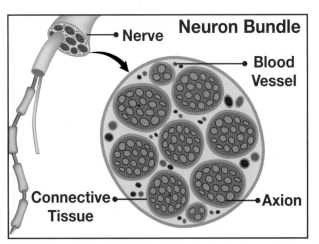

Neuron Bundle

Nerve

Blood Vessel

Connective Tissue

Axion

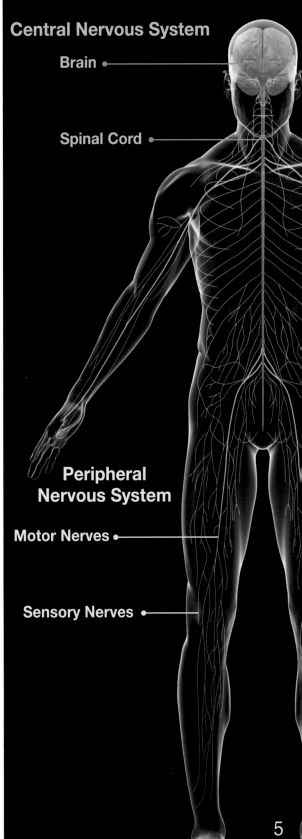

Central Nervous System

Brain

Spinal Cord

Peripheral Nervous System

Motor Nerves

Sensory Nerves

Two kinds of neurons send messages. Sensory neurons carry messages from the senses to the brain and back. Motor neurons carry messages from the brain to muscle fibers and back.

A third kind of neuron is association neurons. They communicate with other neurons in the brain and spinal cord. They let people think, remember, and understand their surroundings. The brain is constantly managing, directing, or storing the incoming and outgoing information.

A neuron ends with branched strands called **dendrites**. The dendrites receive signals from other neurons and relay them to the cell body. The nucleus in the cell body is like a miniature brain. It directs cell actions.

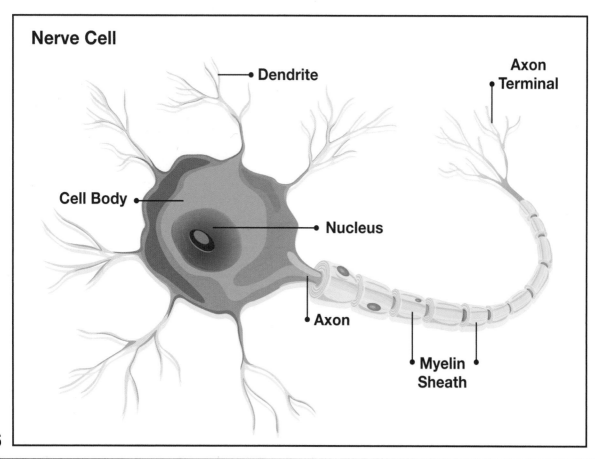

Nerve Cell

Dendrite

Axon Terminal

Cell Body

Nucleus

Axon

Myelin Sheath

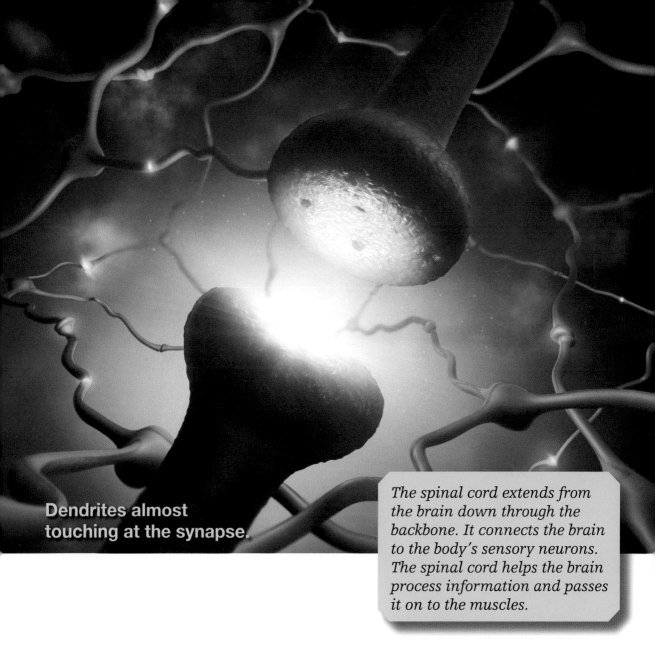

Dendrites almost touching at the synapse.

The spinal cord extends from the brain down through the backbone. It connects the brain to the body's sensory neurons. The spinal cord helps the brain process information and passes it on to the muscles.

The **axon** also holds branched endings. It transmits signals away from the neuron. Neurons don't touch. A tiny gap called a **synapse** keeps them from touching, like the spaces along a sidewalk.

Chemicals send the impulse across the synapse to the dendrites of the next neuron, much like a spark from static electricity shoots from a hand to a doorknob before touching it. The leftover chemicals reabsorb after the message is sent.

THE BRAIN

The brain manages all the information necessary for running the body. It acts like a personal supercomputer to store and bring up thoughts, feelings, emotions, behavior, perception, and memories. The brain also receives information about what the body is doing and what is happening to it. It processes this information and stores it until needed. However, the brain is better than a computer at managing peoples' daily life activities.

The nervous system runs the body. All the parts work together to send, connect, and receive signals over the network of neurons. Living takes constant information— and that takes a brain.

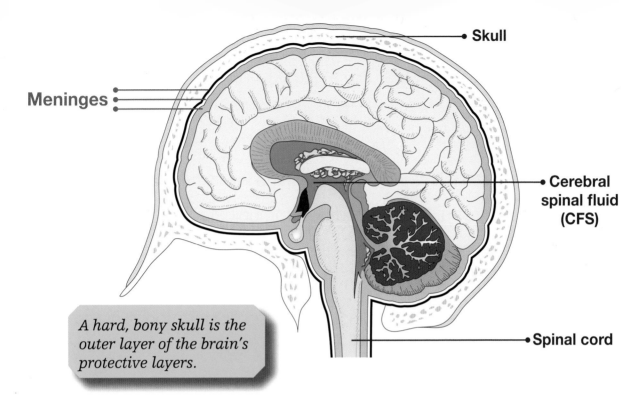

Skull

Men">

Cerebral
spinal fluid
(CFS)

Spinal cord

A hard, bony skull is the outer layer of the brain's protective layers.

The soft brain needs protection. Three strong membranes called **meninges** cover the brain. Fluid called cerebral spinal fluid, or CFS, fills the spaces between the layers. It cushions and protects the brain. CFS also carries hormones, or special body chemicals, around the brain and moves wastes to the blood.

Neurons carry messages and connections made in the brain. **Myelin**, an insulating cover, wraps around axons of many neurons. Myelin moves the messages faster. The impulses jump across the axon instead of traveling along its entire length.

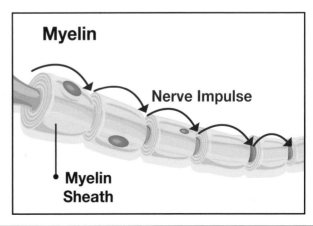

Myelin

Nerve Impulse

Myelin Sheath

Glia cells provide support for the neurons. They don't carry nerve impulses. They make myelin, clean up the spaces, and transport nutrients. Glia cells help make new neuron connections as the brain grows.

The brain is divided into two hemispheres. The right hemisphere mostly controls the left side of the body. The left hemisphere mostly controls the right side. The two sides communicate through a band of connecting axons.

The brain has three main parts. The large cerebrum directs learning, memory, and understanding. A deep center groove divides it into two halves.

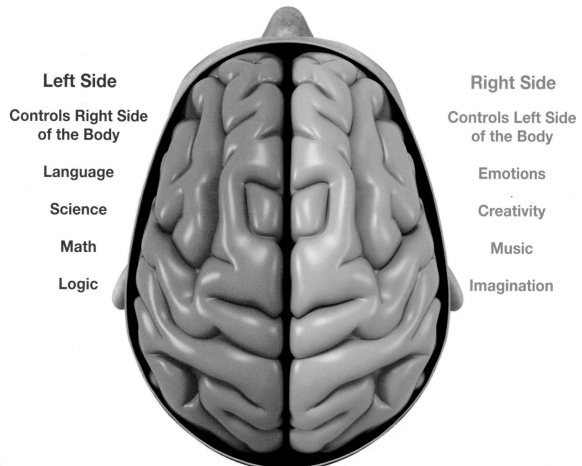

Left Side

Controls Right Side of the Body

Language

Science

Math

Logic

Right Side

Controls Left Side of the Body

Emotions

Creativity

Music

Imagination

The cerebellum sits under the cerebrum at the base of the brain. It controls balance and posture. It also coordinates muscle movements. The cerebellum sends messages to the spinal cord and other parts in the brain.

The brain stem is a stalk-like section deep inside the brain's center. The brain stem

- **Cerebrum**
- **Cerebellum**
- **Brain Stem**

The brain stem is a group of structures leading to the spinal cord.

regulates body actions that take place automatically, like breathing. It also manages vital activities, including maintaining body temperature and sleeping.

Albert Einstein's Brain

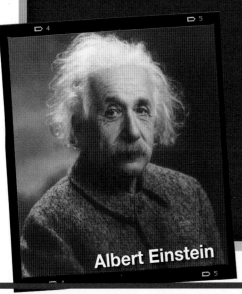

Albert Einstein

Albert Einstein's brain weighed a bit less than a normal brain, but he had a 15% larger region that is associated with visual and spatial reasoning. He also had one large section in the front rather than the several lobes most people do. Einstein's brain was stolen from his dead body and cut apart for study. Before the thief died, he returned it to the hospital from where he'd taken it.

The Cerebral Cortex

The cerebral cortex is the outside part of the cerebrum's surface. It is heavily folded, which gives the brain more surface area. The cerebral cortex is what makes people different from other life forms, like chimpanzees, cats, or frogs. People have a larger cerebral cortex. Its job is thought, speech, and movement processing.

Emotions cause sensory neurons to tell the brain what is happening at that time. The cortex thinks it over and decides how to act in a second.

Did You Know?

During sleep, electrical signals continue, organizing and making sense of the day's information. Four stages of sleep form a cycle that includes a dreaming stage. Scientists don't know for certain why, but everyone dreams.

Frontal Lobe
Intelligence
Reasoning
Behavior
Memory

Parietal Lobe
Intelligence
Language
Sensation
Reading

Temporal Lobe
Hearing
Smell
Memory
Emotions

Occipital Lobe
Vision

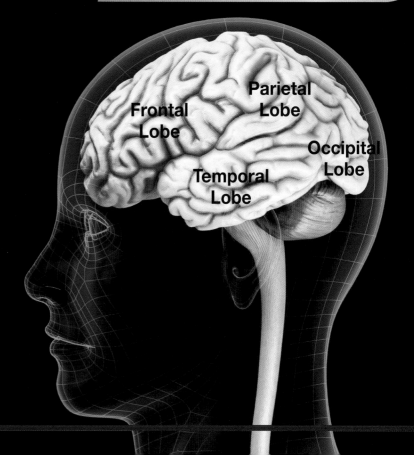

Frontal Lobe

Parietal Lobe

Occipital Lobe

Temporal Lobe

The Thalamus and Hypothalamus

The top of the brain stem holds the thalamus and hypothalamus. The thalamus relays nerve impulses coming from the body. It sends them to the correct brain part. The hypothalamus manages incoming hormones.

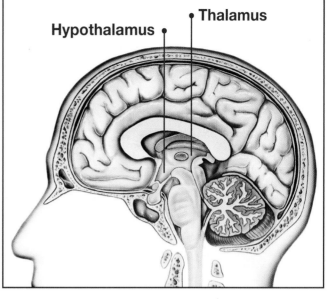

The nervous system develops early in life. By seven weeks, a person's brain is formed. It continues to grow up to birth, and then continues growing. Even as an adult, the brain can develop neurons and form new connections.

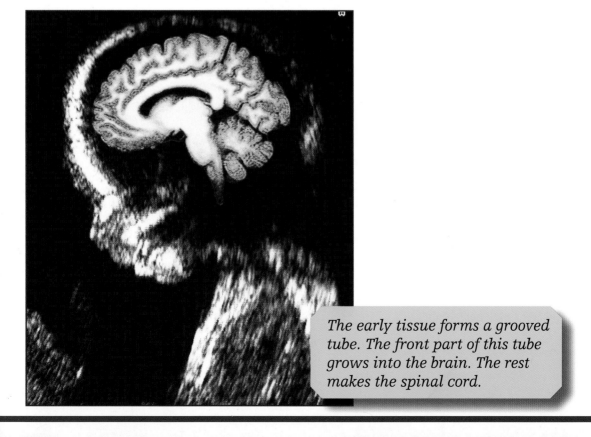

The early tissue forms a grooved tube. The front part of this tube grows into the brain. The rest makes the spinal cord.

13

Babies are born with many neurons that aren't connected. Experiences increase the connections and form the synapses, the spaces between the neurons. Connections grow stronger with each experience. Along the way, unused connections are removed.

The ability of the brain to continue making neurons and connections is **plasticity**. As people age, the process may slow. However, the brain continues to work and repair itself in ways not yet completely understood.

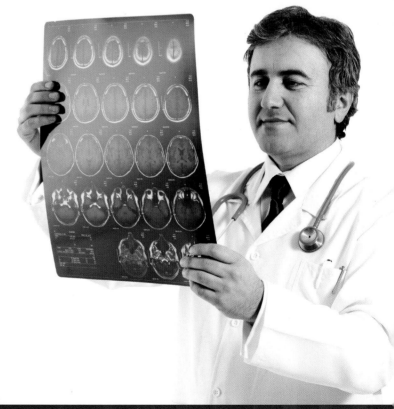

People can't process everything the senses give at once. They pay attention to parts of the information and recall it a bit later. This is sensory memory. Even if someone wasn't paying attention to a question, they might be able to answer it.

Memory appears to be in the connections made by neurons. People receive information, store it, and call it back in long-term memory. Short-term memory lets people remember small information bits. They forget it soon unless they practice it.

The brain runs the body, working with the spinal cord and neurons to receive information from the senses, analyze it, and take needed action.

THE SPINAL CORD

All vertebrate animals have a backbone. Individual bones called **vertebra** stack to form the spinal column. The spinal cord runs from the brain downward through an opening in the center of each bone. These important vertebrae create a tube to protect the thick, cable-like cord.

Small cartilage cushions, or disks, fit between the bones. Fluid fills the remaining space. The spine can flex but still leaves room for 31 pairs of spinal nerves to extend from it throughout the body.

Disks between the vertebrae are made of the same material that forms your nose and ear lobes.

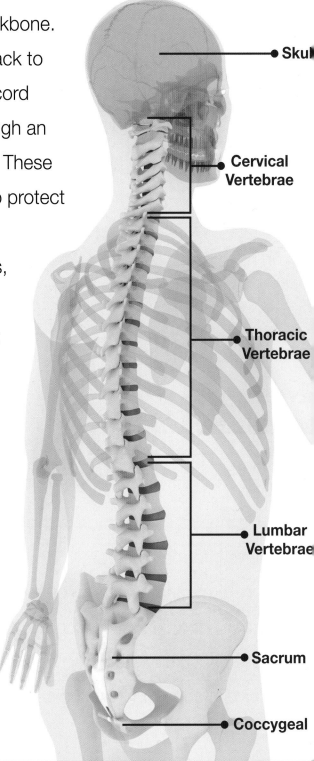

Skull

Cervical
Vertebrae

Thoracic
Vertebrae

Lumbar
Vertebrae

Sacrum

Coccygeal

Information from the senses travels upward through the spinal cord to the brain. The brain sends back information through the spinal cord to the rest of the body.

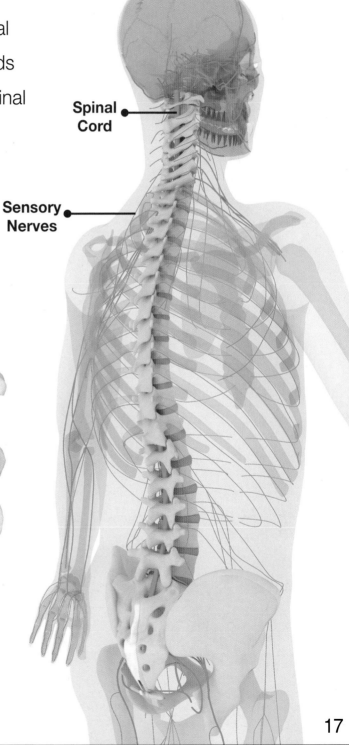

Spinal Cord

Sensory Nerves

Spinal Cord

Cartilage

Sensory Nerve

17

Ever touched a hot pan? A message quickly told the muscles to pull back from the hot object—fast! This is a **reflex**. Reflexes go from sensory neurons to the spinal cord and back to the muscle.

Reflexes shorten the time it takes to deliver a message. The brain learns of it a few seconds after the reflex action. Reflexes protect the body from harm and maintain balance and posture.

Hop on a skateboard. What keeps a skater moving on the board? The brain and spinal cord spring to action to identify balance, move the right muscles, and notice the events taking place. It's the branched nerves in the lower hips and legs that send the messages about the skater's movements.

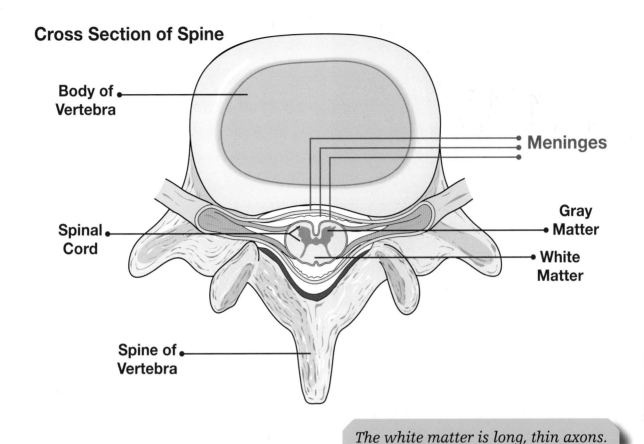

Cross Section of Spine

Body of
Vertebra

Meninges

Spinal
Cord

Gray
Matter

White
Matter

Spine of
Vertebra

The white matter is long, thin axons. They carry the electrical nerve impulses to other neurons.

Tissues that protect the brain also protect the spinal cord. Meninges wrap the cord in three layers. CSF like that in the brain fills the spaces around the cord. It protects the cord by absorbing shocks. CSF has minerals and oxygen that sustain the spinal cord.

Gray matter in the spinal cord forms the main part of the nerve cell bodies and their branched dendrite endings. This matter receives messages from the body and sends them to the brain. The brain sends messages to the body through these nerves.

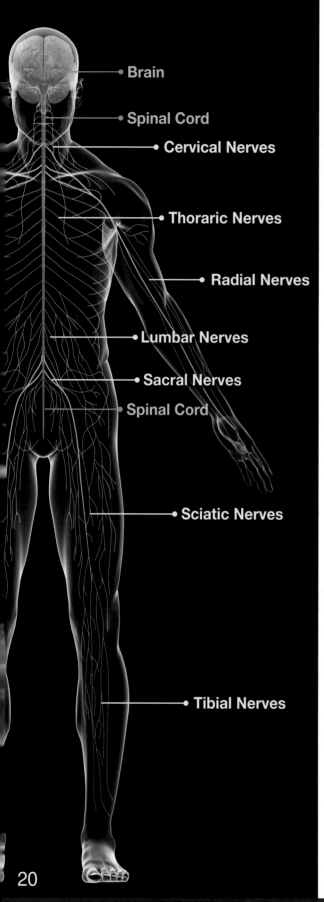

- Brain
- Spinal Cord
- Cervical Nerves
- Thoraric Nerves
- Radial Nerves
- Lumbar Nerves
- Sacral Nerves
- Spinal Cord
- Sciatic Nerves
- Tibial Nerves

Sensory messages leave the sense organs and travel to the brain through the spinal cord. Internal sensors control activities like maintaining body temperature and blood pressure.

Motor messages travel from the brain through the spinal cord to the body. They tell the muscles what to do. Others control organs that run the body and glands like saliva. This set of body nerves forms the PNS.

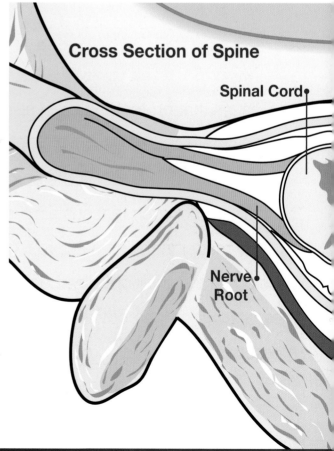

Cross Section of Spine

Spinal Cord

Nerve Root

The spinal nerves have roots divided in two parts. One part goes back, and the other curves forward. The two sets of roots carry separate messages. The back nerve root sends sensory messages to the cord. The front nerve root gives motor nerve information headed to muscles and glands.

The nervous system acts as a message center. This system controls every action needed to live.

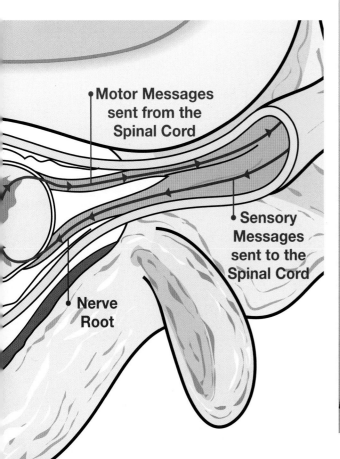

Motor Messages sent from the Spinal Cord

Sensory Messages sent to the Spinal Cord

Nerve Root

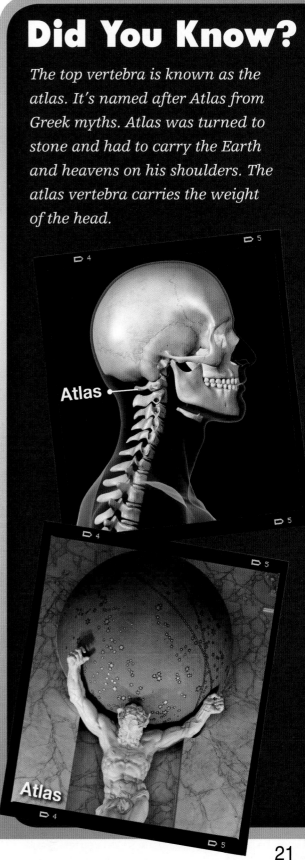

Did You Know?

The top vertebra is known as the atlas. It's named after Atlas from Greek myths. Atlas was turned to stone and had to carry the Earth and heavens on his shoulders. The atlas vertebra carries the weight of the head.

Atlas

Atlas

THE SENSES

Touch

Petting a puppy feels different than rubbing a finger across sandpaper. Yet feeling each is processed the same way.

Sensors in the skin detect what a person is touching. That information triggers

a message that moves to the brain or spinal cord in an electrical impulse. The brain takes the information. It informs the senses what it is touching and instructs the body what to do. It all happens in an instant.

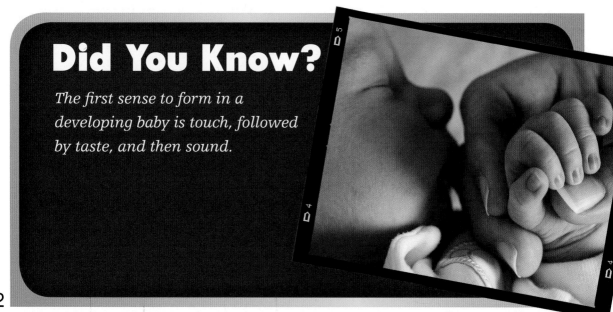

Did You Know?

The first sense to form in a developing baby is touch, followed by taste, and then sound.

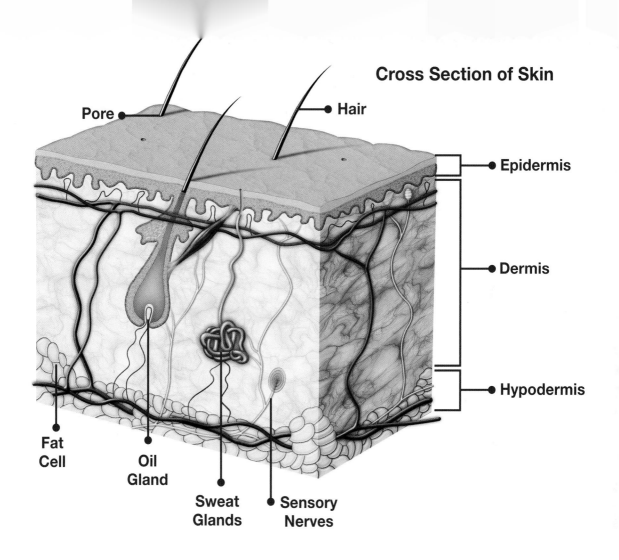

Cross Section of Skin

Pore

Hair

Epidermis

Dermis

Hypodermis

Fat Cell

Oil Gland

Sweat Glands

Sensory Nerves

What's the largest organ in the human body? Everyone can see it, too! It's the skin and it is formed of layers. The **epidermis** is the top layer. The **dermis** is under the epidermis. The touch sensors, along with blood vessels, sweat glands, hair openings, and oil glands lie in the dermis. A deeper layer underneath protects the body like a shock absorber.

Hot

Cold

Pain

Sensors for heat, cold, and pain come off branched nerve endings. These sensors cover the body, but places like lips and hands have more.

A touch signals a chemical change that starts the message to the nerve. The nerves pass along the touch sensations to the cerebrum. The brain forms an image giving information about what it is touching. The information protects the body or makes it feel good.

Did You Know?

People feel their clothing when they first get dressed. They quickly become used to the feel and no longer notice it after a short time.

Sight

Look at a snow-covered mountain. How do people's eyes see the colors and differences in the sky and snow? Sight involves using the eyes for sensory information. The inside of the eyeball holds special receptors that

respond to light. The pupils change sizes to control the amount of light coming in.

Two receptors called cones and rods identify shapes and colors. After light hits the cones and rods, a chemical change triggers an electrical signal. The neurons from these receptors combine to make a thick, cable-like nerve called the optic nerve. The nerve runs to the brain's visual area. The brain forms a 3-D picture using the optic nerve's impulses.

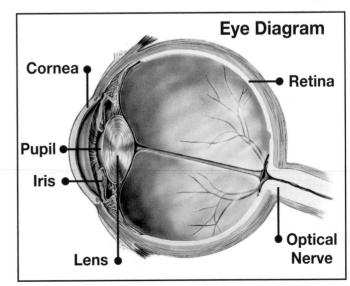

Eye Diagram

Cornea

Retina

Pupil

Iris

Lens

Optical Nerve

Sound

A whisper or thunderclap make different sounds. People hear using their ears, but how does that work? Sound moves through the air by vibrations. These vibrations enter the ear. Sounds enter the outer ear and

move the eardrum that separates the outer and middle ear. The air-filled middle ear passes along the eardrum vibrations. These vibrations move a set of tiny bones. A tube from the middle ear runs to the throat.

The inner ear holds a spiral, fluid-filled canal called the cochlea. The sound vibrations put pressure on hair-like receptors, or **cilia**, in the cochlea. Each hair has a nerve at its base. Pressure moves the hair. This sets off the impulses, which travel through the cochlear nerve to

Ear Diagram

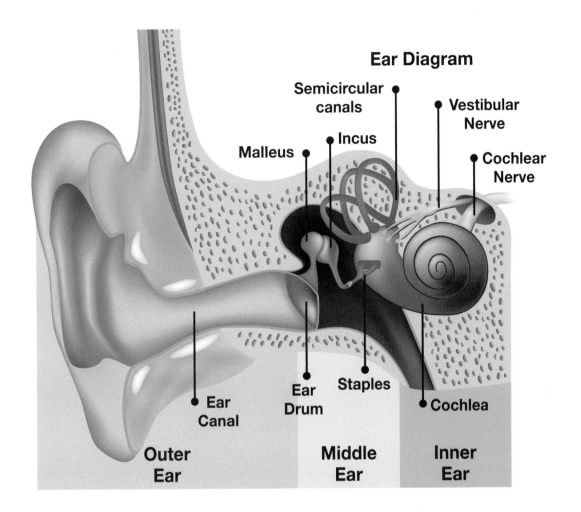

- Semicircular canals
- Vestibular Nerve
- Incus
- Cochlear Nerve
- Malleus
- Ear Canal
- Ear Drum
- Staples
- Cochlea

Outer Ear **Middle Ear** **Inner Ear**

The inner ear also holds receptors for balance. Fluid inside tubes moves when the head moves. The receptor hairs send the brain information to tell where the correct balance lies.

Infections in the ear upset the pressures there, resulting in pain or dizziness.

Taste and Smell

The brain combines the information sent by the taste and smell senses. Sense receptors work together to identify tastes and smells.

Hungry? Dig in to a meal! It's the brain that identifies how food tastes. Taste buds on the tongue recognize sweet, salty, sour, bitter, and a savory, meaty taste called **umami**. Little holes in taste buds on the sides of tiny bumps detect dissolved food chemicals. The receptors in the taste buds then send nerve impulses to the brain.

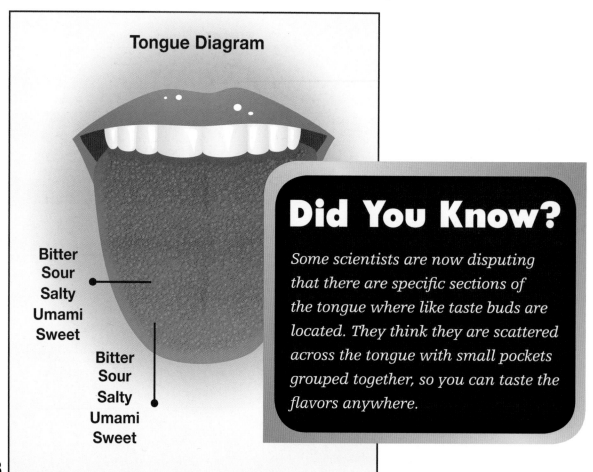

Tongue Diagram

Bitter
Sour
Salty
Umami
Sweet

Bitter
Sour
Salty
Umami
Sweet

Did You Know?

Some scientists are now disputing that there are specific sections of the tongue where like taste buds are located. They think they are scattered across the tongue with small pockets grouped together, so you can taste the flavors anywhere.

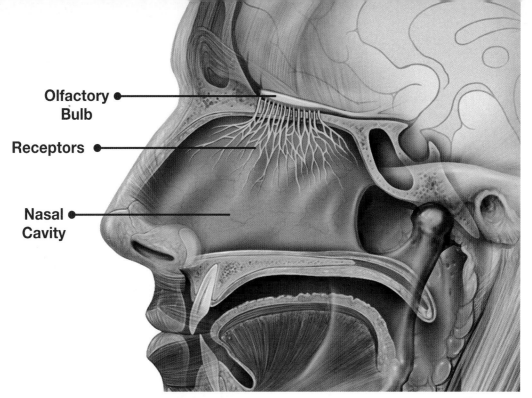

Olfactory Bulb

Receptors

Nasal Cavity

Ever had a stuffy nose? Air moves up the nose with each breath. Smell receptors with brush-like cilia sit in the upper cavity of the nose. The smell molecules dissolve in mucus and attach to the cilia. They trigger nerve endings which move to a special sensory bulb. This sends the impulses through a nerve to the brain region that controls smell. A stuffy nose prevents the smells from moving up the nose. That's why food tastes different when you have a cold.

WHEN THINGS GO WRONG

Sturdy bones and fluid help protect the brain and spinal cord. However, injuries, accidents, and illness do happen. Serious physical harm causes **trauma**. Trauma often results from drowning, choking, suffocating, heart attacks, carbon monoxide poisoning, or head injuries. These injuries may cut off oxygen to the brain. After several minutes without oxygen, brain cells begin to die. Brain death happens when no electrical impulses place.

Did You Know?

A blow to the head or body causes the brain to rattle inside the skull. This motion stretches the brain, damaging cells and causing chemical changes to happen inside. Concussions can occur in football, even to young players. You can't see a concussion, but doctors must look for signs of one.

Concussion symptoms include blurry vision, dizziness, and behavior changes.

A stroke happens when blood to part of the brain is stopped. A blood vessel can break. Blood floods the cells around it. A blood clot may block the blood vessel. Either way, the cells lose oxygen and die. The body region controlled by that part of the brain doesn't work.

Numbness or weakness on one side, vision or speech problems, confusion, and loss of balance can mean a stroke. Treatments include controlling diseases leading to strokes and using clot-dissolving medicines.

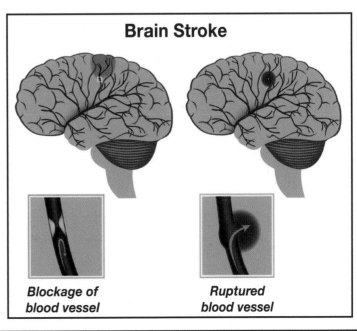

Brain Stroke

Blockage of blood vessel

Ruptured blood vessel

Dementia is a group of brain symptoms where functioning memory and thought is lost. Alzheimer's is a brain disorder causing neuron connections to break down. Proteins not usually found in the brain collect there. Over time, mental function lessens. No treatment can stop it, but some medicines slow its progress.

Spina bifida is a group of disorders. It happens when the grooved tube forming the brain doesn't close properly. It also causes problems in the spinal cord. Symptoms can be mild or severe. Sometimes muscle control is lost.

Viruses or bacteria can infect the brain, spinal cord, or the meninges around the nerve cells. These infections can cause serious swelling which causes damaging pressure. Many infections can be treated.

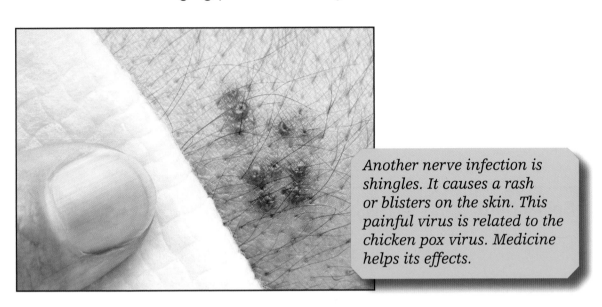

Another nerve infection is shingles. It causes a rash or blisters on the skin. This painful virus is related to the chicken pox virus. Medicine helps its effects.

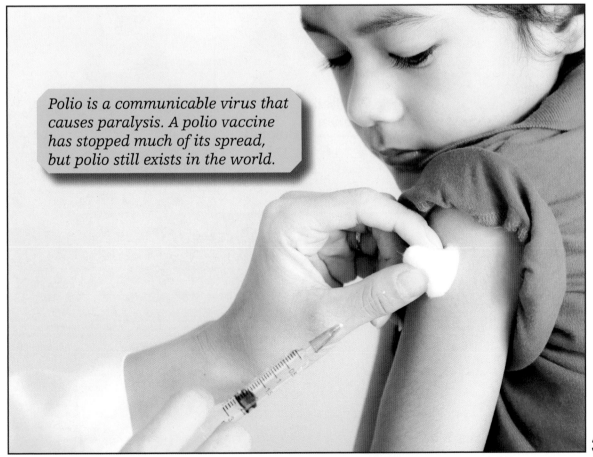

Polio is a communicable virus that causes paralysis. A polio vaccine has stopped much of its spread, but polio still exists in the world.

The disks between vertebrae can press on the spinal cord, triggering nerves that cause pain. Sometimes disks crack. The inner cartilage squeezes out. This pressure on the spinal cord causes pain. Medicine, therapy, and sometimes surgery help.

Most spinal cord injuries don't cut the cord entirely. Crushed or out of line vertebrae injure the cord's axons. Any disruption of the message path from an injury stops the signal from continuing on its path.

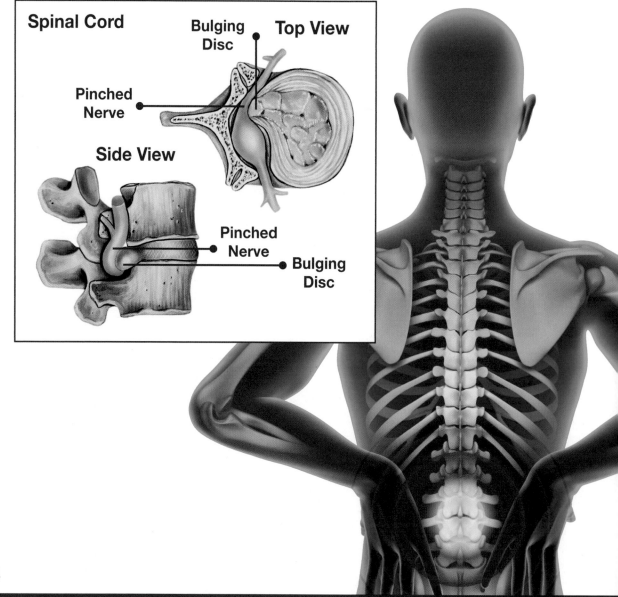

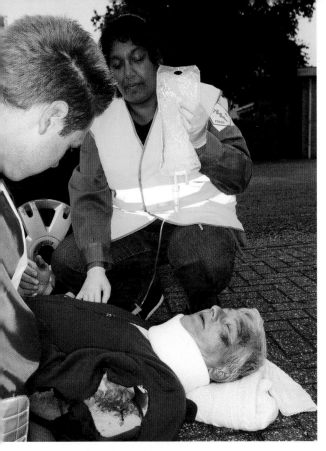

Medical treatment within eight hours of a spinal cord injury improves the chance of recovery. But cord damage in the neck regions can cause paralysis. Don't move a person who might have spinal cord damage. Get help.

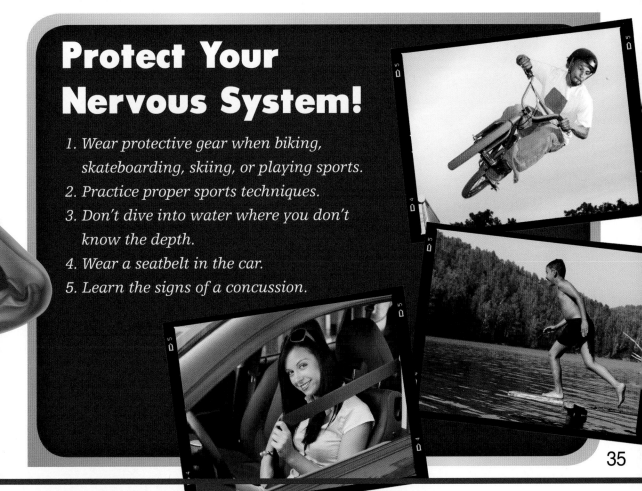

Protect Your Nervous System!

1. *Wear protective gear when biking, skateboarding, skiing, or playing sports.*
2. *Practice proper sports techniques.*
3. *Don't dive into water where you don't know the depth.*
4. *Wear a seatbelt in the car.*
5. *Learn the signs of a concussion.*

Motor neuron diseases destroy cells that control muscle actions. MS (multiple sclerosis) and ALS (amyotrophic lateral sclerosis), also known as Lou Gehrig's disease, cause the muscles to

waste away. There is no cure for these diseases now.

Parkinson's disease is a motor system disorder originating in the brain. It interferes with chemical signals that direct the muscles. Symptoms include trembling and lack of coordination. There is no cure, but treatments may help symptoms.

Actor Michael J. Fox was diagnosed with Parkinson's disease in 1991. His positive outlook and desire to educate people about the disease and to find a cure led him to create the Michael J. Fox Foundation, where he hopes to close the gap between current research and treating people with the disease.

The nervous system performs multiple activities that keep people going about their lives. When things go wrong, it causes major disruptions in the body's messaging ability. However, thanks to groundbreaking research, the future holds hope for people with nervous system disorders.

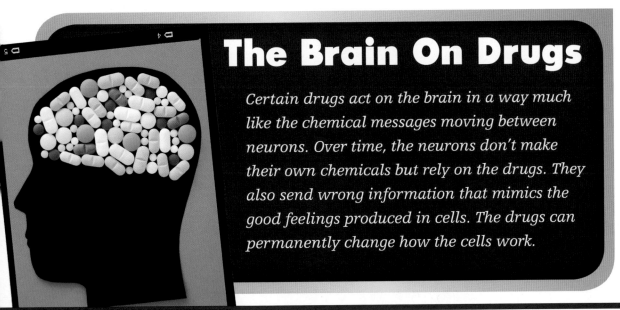

The Brain On Drugs

Certain drugs act on the brain in a way much like the chemical messages moving between neurons. Over time, the neurons don't make their own chemicals but rely on the drugs. They also send wrong information that mimics the good feelings produced in cells. The drugs can permanently change how the cells work.

FOR THE FUTURE

Neurologists treat problems with the nervous system. They look at body symptoms for signs of problems in the nervous system.

Scans are one way doctors see problems. CT scans make a 3-D image of the brain. MRI scans use magnetism to form an image to study. X-rays show broken vertebrae. PET scans use special chemicals injected into the body that are seen on X-rays. These tools help doctors identify the problem area.

Name that Machine

Names of machines *(Abbreviation)*
computerized tomography (CT)
magnetic resonance imaging (MRI)
positron emission tomography (PET)
global positioning systems (GPS)
brain-computer interfacing (BCI)
functional magnetic resonance imaging (FMRI)

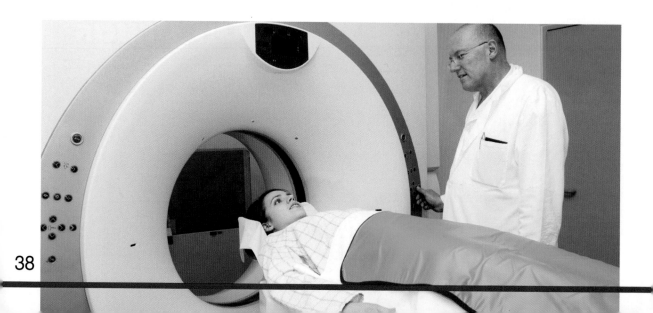

Computer guided robotics may aid surgeons when performing delicate surgery.

Severe brain injuries sometimes need surgery to repair the damage. Surgeons operate to remove tumors and perform brain surgery using microscopes. 3-D microscopes help them see the nerve bundles better. Tiny tools allow exact cuts. Laser scalpels both cut and seal off small areas. Using imaging, doctors can tell healthy tissue from the problem areas.

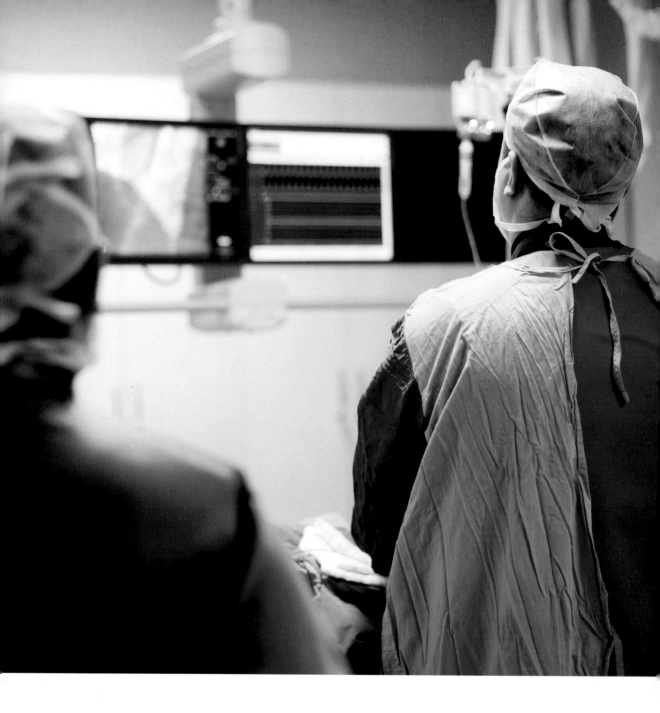

Doctors use technology like GPS to guide small tools through blood vessels. The tools work with scans that pass through a computer. A 3-D image forms, letting them pinpoint the problem. Turning the computerized image lets doctors see all parts of the healthy brain.

Neuron research is continuing to make discoveries. New studies are looking at how firing specific neurons might aid hearing loss. Others work to understand changes in neurons during intense and long-term pain. Other studies involve transplanting glia cells to treat ALS and at ways of improving the interaction between neurons and artificial body extensions, like arms and legs.

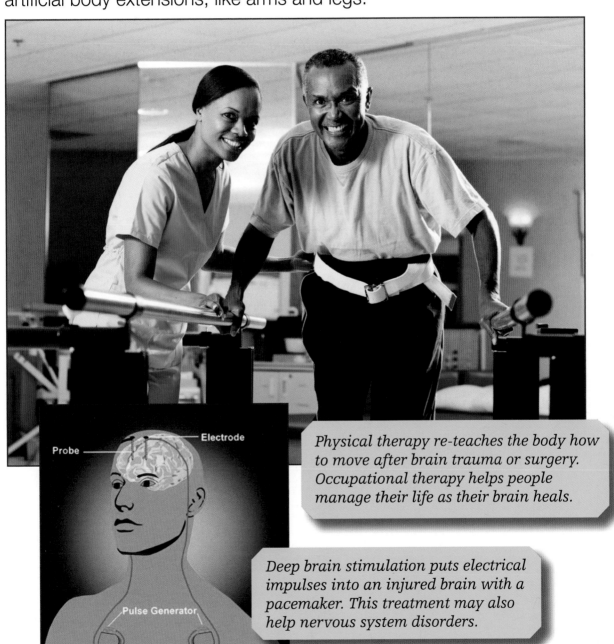

Probe

Electrode

Pulse Generator

Physical therapy re-teaches the body how to move after brain trauma or surgery. Occupational therapy helps people manage their life as their brain heals.

Deep brain stimulation puts electrical impulses into an injured brain with a pacemaker. This treatment may also help nervous system disorders.

Technology like brain-computer interfacing (BCI) lets people control thoughts to direct computers, robots, and virtual reality environments. The system catches brain signals and creates commands. Patients who are paralyzed will use their thoughts to move cursors. They will be able to control computers, robotic arms, and wheelchairs.

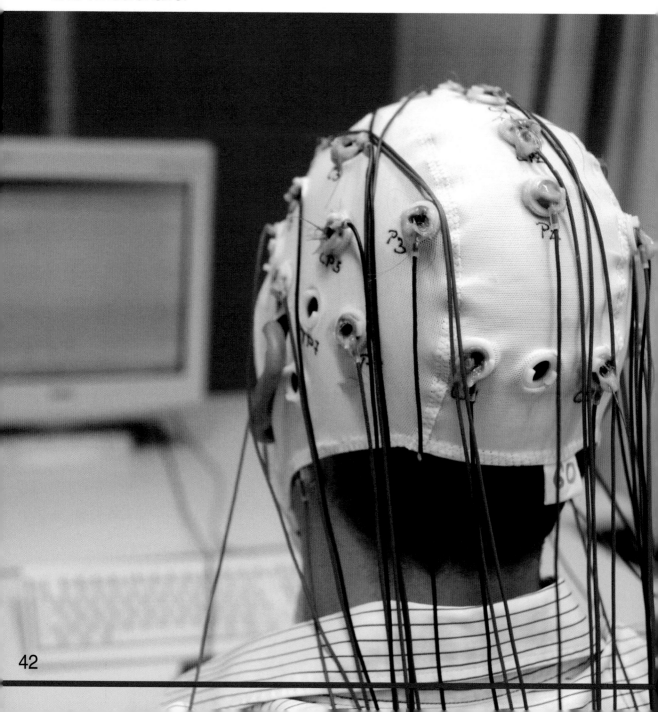

Studies of society's influence on brains and early childhood activities continue to bring new information. Studies have found that remaining social as people age keeps brains active.

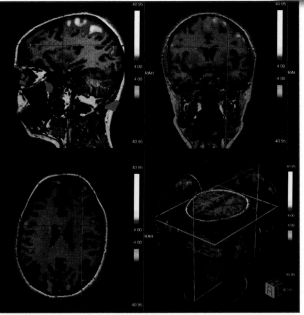

Functional magnetic resonance imaging (FMRI) show neuron activity in the blood's oxygen. This lets doctors map mental activity by showing changes in the brain's blood flow.

New genetics research offers memory and recognition treatments. Scientists have knocked out a gene for an enzyme to study what part a specific protein plays in developing dementia. Since brain disorders often happen at the synapses, another study is using optogenetics. This turns off and on brain cells genetically, using pulses of light to study synapses. Stem cell and glia cell research may lead to cures for diseases.

Dendrites almost touching at the synapse.

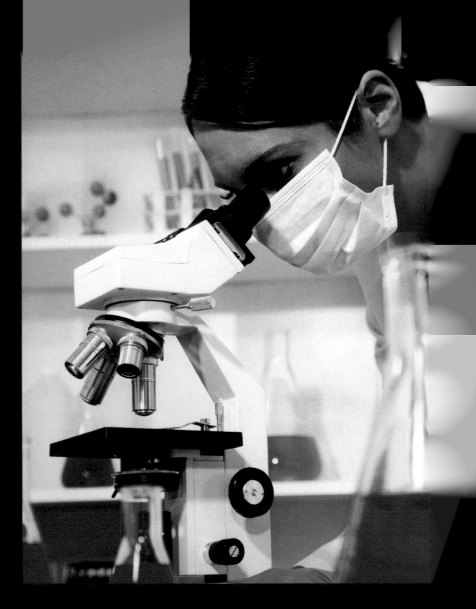

Research will answer many questions about the nervous system in the future. Scientists and doctors who are studying diseases, pain relief, mental illness, and trauma may help find cures for multiple disorders. In coming years, new research will certainly provide more information to help understand this complex system.

GLOSSARY

axon (AK-sohn): the branched endings in a nerve cell that transmits signals away from the cell

central nervous system (SEN-truhl NUR-vuhs SIS-tuhm): the brain and spinal cord

cilia (SIL-ee-uh): tiny, hair-like structures in the human body that wave to pass along vibrations or particles

dendrites (DEN-drites): the branched nerve endings that receive signals from other nerve cells

dermis (DUHR-muhs): the layer of skin lying beneath the epidermis

epidermis (EP-i-durh-muhs): the outer layer of the skin

glia (GLEE-uh): cells in the nervous system that support neurons

impulses (IM-puhls-iz): the electrical signals sent along neurons

meninges (muh-NIN-jeez): tough membranes covering the organs of the nervous system

myelin (MYE-uh-lihn): an insulating cover on neurons to speed the signals

neurologists (nuhr-AWH-luh-jists): doctors who specialize in the
problems with the nervous system

neurons (NUHR-ahns): nerve cells

peripheral nervous system (puh-RIF-uhr-uhl NUR-vuhs SIS-tuhm):
all the nerves outside the brain and spinal cord

plasticity (plas-TI-sit-ee): the ability of the brain to form new
neurons and connections

reflex (REE-fleks): an automatic action resulting from nerves going
through the spinal cord, bypassing the brain

spinal cord (SPINE-uhl kord): the thick bundle of nerves down the
backbone that carries messages between the body and the brain

synapse (SIN-ahps): the gap between nerve cells

trauma (TRAW-muh): severe injury

umami (yoo-MAH-mee): the taste bud producing a savory, meat-like
taste

vertebra(e) (VUR-tuh-bruh); plural VUR-tuh-bray): the bones found
in the backbone that protect the spinal cord

INDEX

axons   6, 7, 9, 10, 19, 20, 34

brain stem   11, 13

central nervous system   5

cerebellum   11

cerebral cortex   12

cerebrum   10, 11, 24

dendrites   6, 7

diseases of nervous system   31, 36, 44, 45

hemispheres   10

peripheral nervous system   5

reflex   18

scans   38, 40

senses   6, 15, 17, 22, 28, 29

spinal cord   4-7, 11, 15-20, 22, 30, 32-35

trauma   30, 41, 45

vertebrae   16, 34, 38

WEBSITES TO VISIT

www.pbs.org/wnet/brain/illusions/form.html

faculty.washington.edu/chudler/neurok.html

www.dana.org/resources/brainykids/

ABOUT THE AUTHOR

Shirley Duke is a writer and former teacher. She is the author of many nonfiction books and enjoys writing about science, which is a little like teaching science. She is interested how living things work. She lives in Texas and in the Jemez Mountains of New Mexico.

Ask The Author!
www.rem4students.com